Disney Surname

Ireland: 1600s to 1900s

From Ireland Church Records of Baptism, Marriage and Death

Comprised of Roman Catholic and Church of Ireland Records

From Counties Carlow, Cork, Kerry and Dublin City

Compiled by **Donovan Hurst**

March 14, 2013

Dedication

This work is dedicated to all of those that came before us and shaped our lives to make us the people that we are today.

Table of Contents

Introduction

This is a compilation of individuals who have the surname of Disney that lived in the country of Ireland from the 1600s to the 1900s. I have placed each entry into one of four categories: Families, Individual Births/Baptisms, Individual Burials, and Individual Marriages. If a marriage entry primarily concerns an Individual Disney whom is female, then I have placed that entry under the category of Individual Marriages. If a marriage entry primarily concerns an Individual Disney whom is male, then I have placed that entry under the category of Families. Images of many of these listings are available at http://churchrecords.irishgenealogy.ie/churchrecords/.

To help guide the reader of this work, the format of this book is as follows:

- Main Family Entry (Husband and Wife) (Father and Mother)

  - Child of Main Family Entry, including Spouse(s) when available

    - Grandchild of Main Family Entry, including Spouse(s) when available

    - Great-Grandchild of Main Family Entry, including Spouse(s) when available

(**Bolded Text**) following any entry includes any additional information such as Residence(s), Occupation(s), Signature(s), etc. when available.

Hurst

Some of the fonts used in this work symbolizes Celtic writing. The traditional letters, numbers, and punctuation marks and their Celtic counterparts are as follows:

Traditional Letters (Uppercase & Lowercase)

A a B b C c D d E f G g H h I i J j K k L l M m N n O o P p Q q R r S s T t U u V v W w X x Y y Z z

Celtic Letters (Uppercase & Lowercase)

A a B b C c D ð E e F ƒ G g H h I í J j K k L l M m

N n O o P p Q q R r S s T t U u V v W w X x Y y Z z

Traditional Numbers

1 2 3 4 5 6 7 8 9 10

Celtic Numbers

1 2 3 4 5 6 7 8 9 10

Traditional Punctuation

. , : ' " & - ( )

Celtic Punctuation

. , : ' " & - ( )

Parish Churches

Carlow (Church of Ireland)

Carlow Parish, Dunleckney Parish, Old Leighlin Parish, and Tullow Parish.

Cork & Ross (Roman Catholic or RC)

Skibbereen (Creagh & Sullon) Parish.

Dublin (Church of Ireland)

Clontarf Parish, Crumlin Parish, Irishtown Parish, Rathmines Parish, St. Andrew Parish, St. Anne Parish, St. Audoen Parish, St. Bride Parish, St. Catherine Parish, St. George Parish, St. James Parish, St. John Parish, St. Luke Parish, St. Mark Parish, St. Mary Parish, St. Matthew Parish, St. Michael Parish, St. Michan Parish, St. Nicholas Without Parish, St. Paul Parish, St. Peter Parish, St. Stephen Parish, St. Thomas Parish, and St. Werburgh Parish.

Dublin (Roman Catholic or RC)

Clondalkin Parish, Harrington Street Parish, Rathmines Parish, St. Andrew Parish, St. Audoen Parish, St. Catherine Parish, St. Mary, Pro Cathedral Parish, and St. Nicholas Parish.

Kerry (Church of Ireland)

Ballymacelligott Parish, Ballymacelligott & Ballyseedy Parish, Kilcolman Parish, Kilgobbin Parish, and Tralee Parish.

Families

- Charles Disney & Mary Thorpe – 27 Feb 1816 (Marriage, **St. Audoen Parish**)

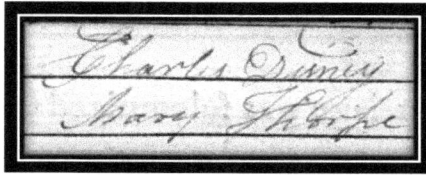

Signatures:

- o Margaret Disney – b. 22 Dec 1818, bapt. 3 Jan 1819 (Baptism, **St. Audoen Parish**)

- o Margaret Disney – b. 23 Mar 1822, bapt. 1 Sep 1822 (Baptism, **St. Audoen Parish**)

- o Charlotte Disney – b. 26 Sep 1823, bapt. 26 Dec 1823 (Baptism, **St. Peter Parish**)

- o John Disney – b. 1824, bur. 13 Mar 1825 (Burial, **St. Audoen Parish**)

John Disney (son):

Residence - St. Audoen Parish - before March 13, 1825

Age at Death - 1 year

- o Elizabeth Disney – b. 1 May 1825, bapt. 3 Jul 1825 (Baptism, **St. Audoen Parish**)

Charles Disney (father):

Residence - St. Mary Parish - February 27, 1816

Mary Thorpe (mother):

Residence - St. Audoen Parish - February 27, 1816

Hurst

Wedding Witnesses:

John Thorpe & Benjamin Dill

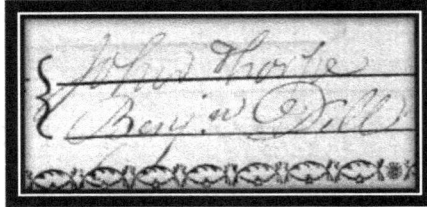

Signatures:

- Edward Ogle Disney & Matilda Disney
  - Edward Henry Disney, b. 5 Oct 1856, bapt. 29 Oct 1856 (Baptism, **St. George Parish**) & Elizabeth Anne Stirling – 27 Jun 1892 (Marriage, **St. George Parish**)

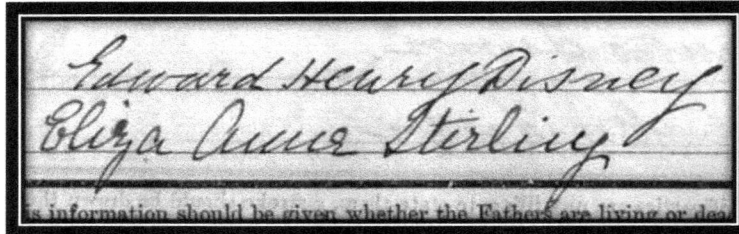

Signatures:

  - Aileen Disney – b. 23 Jul 1896, bapt. 19 Aug 1896 (Baptism, **St. George Parish**)

Edward Henry Disney (son):

Residence - **29 Temple Street** - June **27, 1892**

10 Temple Street - August 19, 1896

Occupation - Gentleman - June 27, 1892

Bank of Ireland Official - August 19, 1896

Disney Surname Ireland: 1600s to 1900s

Elizabeth Anne Stirling, daughter of Hall Stirling (daughter-in-law):

   Residence - 10 Temple Street - June 27, 1892

Hall Stirling (father):

   Occupation - Solicitor

Edward Ogle Disney (father):

   Occupation - Clerk in Holy Orders

Wedding Witnesses:

George Miller Dobbin & William Disney

Signatures:

Edward Ogle Disney (father):

   Residence - 12 Great Denmark Street - October 29, 1856

      Kelleshil, Co. Tyrone - October 29, 1856

   Occupation - Clergyman - October 29, 1856

- Elias Disney & Susan Disney – 26 Oct 1825 (Marriage, Tullow Parish)

Signatures:

Hurst

Elias Disney (husband):

Residence - Clonas, Co. Kilkenny - October 26, 1825

Susan Disney (wife):

Residence - Tullow - October 26, 1825

Wedding Witnesses:

Thomas Disney & John Disney

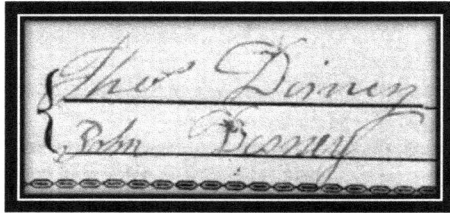

Signatures:

- Fownes Disney & Anne Pendergast – 6 Dec 1788 (Marriage, **St. Bride Parish**)

Fownes Disney (husband):

Occupation - Gentleman - December 6, 1788

Anne Pendergast (wife):

Occupation - Spinster - December 6, 1788

- Francis Disney & Clare Croclois
  - Clare Christine Mary Josephine Disney, b. 10 Feb 1872, bapt. 26 Mar 1880 (Baptism, **St. Nicholas Parish (RC)**) & Peter Chamboissier – 29 May 1889 (Marriage, **Harrington Street Parish (RC)**)
    - Mary Josephine Chamboissier – b. 8 Dec 1891, bapt. 11 Dec 1891 (Baptism, **St. Mary, Pro Cathedral Parish (RC)**), bapt. 1 Jan 1892 (Baptism, **Harrington Street Parish (RC)**)

4

Disney Surname Ireland: 1600s to 1900s

Clare Disney (daughter):

   Residence - 40 Heytesbury Street - May 29, 1889

Peter Chamboissier, son of Eugene Chamboissier & Angela Leonard (son-in-law):

   Residence - 40 Heytesbury Street - Mary 29, 1889

                    January 1, 1892

         Rotunda Hospital - December 11, 1891

Wedding Witnesses:

Arnold Horriey & Louise Garr

Francis Disney (father):

   Residence - Celbridge - March 26, 1880

- Francis Disney & Elizabeth Disney
  - o Francis John Disney – b. 27 Sep 1862, bapt. 8 Oct 1862 (Baptism, **St. Peter Parish**)

Francis Disney (father):

   Residence - No. 45 Rathmines Road - October 8, 1862

   Occupation - Servant - October 8, 1862

- Francis Disney & Unknown
  - o Francis Disney – bapt. 26 Dec 1862 (Baptism, **St. Nicholas Parish (RC)**)

Francis Disney (father):

   Residence - 80 Clanbrassil Street - December 26, 1862

- Francis Disney & Unknown
  - Francis Disney (1st Marriage) & Sarah Jane Burland Johnston – 24 Apr 1873 (Marriage, **St. George Parish**)

Signatures:

- Francis Emmanuel Disney – b. 21 Dec 1874, bapt. 16 Feb 1875 (Baptism, **St. Peter Parish**)
  - Francis Disney (2nd Marriage) & Margaret Cadden Coote – 22 Jun 1889 (Marriage, **St. Stephen Parish**)

Signatures:

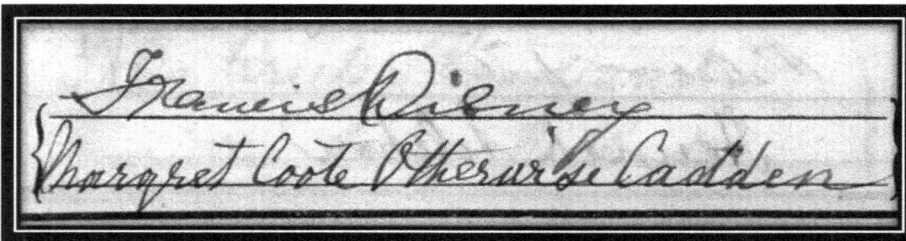

Francis Disney (son-in-law):

Residence - 20 North Summer Street - April 24, 1873

3 Lower Leeson Street - February 16, 1875

13 Holles Street - June 22, 1889

Disney Surname Ireland: 1600s to 1900s

Occupation - Butler - April 24, 1873

House Steward - February 16, 1875

June 22, 1889

Relationship Status at 2nd Marriage - widow

Sarah Burland Johnston, daughter of Joseph S. Burland (1st wife) (daughter-in-law):

Residence - 20 North Summer Street - April 24, 1873

Relationship Status at Marriage - widow

Joseph S. Burland (father):

Occupation - Cabinet Maker

Francis Disney (father):

Occupation - Carpenter

Wedding Witnesses:

James Connall & Moses Cordner

Signatures:

Margaret Cadden Coote, daughter of James Cadden (2nd wife) (daughter-in-law):

Residence - Sir P. Dennis Hospital - June 22, 1889

Relationship Status at Marriage - widow

James Cadden (father):

Occupation - Farmer

Francis Disney (father):

Occupation - Cabinet Maker

Wedding Witnesses:

William Coote & Louise Crumpe

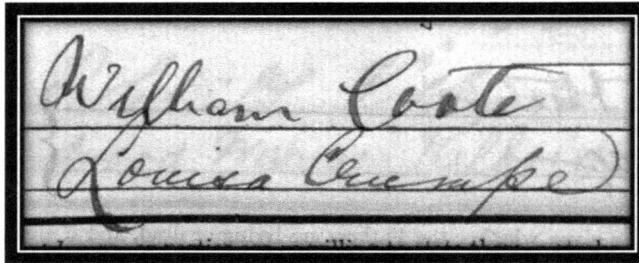

Signatures:

* George Disney & Mary Disney
    * Frances Disney – b. 15 Feb 1723, bapt. 9 Mar 1723 (Baptism, **St. Mary Parish**)
* George Disney & Mary Disney
    * George Disney – bapt. 4 Sep 1797 (Baptism, **Old Leighlin Parish**)
    * Richard Disney – bapt. 3 Jan 1800 (Baptism, **Old Leighlin Parish**)

George Disney (father):

Residence - Wells Parish - September 4, 1797

Disney Surname Ireland: 1600s to 1900s

- Henry Disney & Ellen Unknown

  o Ellen Juliana Disney – b. 23 Jan 1829, bapt. 1 Feb 1829 (Baptism, St. George Parish)

  o William Henry Disney (1st Marriage), b. 19 Apr 1831, bapt. 28 Apr 1831 (Baptism, St. George Parish) & Mary Jane Denny, b. 1832, d. 3 Sep 1864, bur. 3 Sep 1864 (Burial, Ballymacelligott Parish) – 28 Jan 1857 (Marriage, Tralee Parish)

Signatures:

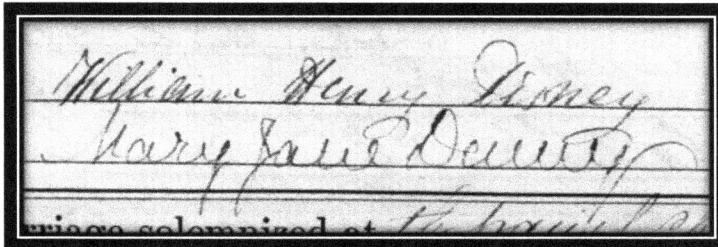

  - Henry William Disney – bapt. 31 Jan 1858 (Baptism, Tralee Parish)

  - Anthony Edward Denny Disney – bapt. 22 Apr 1859 (Baptism, Tralee Parish)

  - Catherine Disney – bapt. 19 Aug 1860 (Baptism, Tralee Parish)

  - William Disney – bapt. 22 Dec 1861 (Baptism, Tralee Parish)

  - Eleanor Disney – b. 21 Jul 1863, bapt. 6 Sep 1863 (Baptism, Ballymacelligott & Ballyseedy Parish)

  - Marie A. Disney – bapt. 6 Oct 1864 (Baptism, Kilgobbin Parish)

  o William Henry Disney (2nd Marriage), b. 19 Apr 1831, bapt. 28 Apr 1831 (Baptism, St. George Parish) & Esther Unknown

  - Robert Baxter Disney – b. 14 Sep 1871, bapt. 22 Oct 1871 (Baptism, Ballymacelligott & Ballyseedy Parish)

  - Esther Wemys Disney – b. 9 Dec 1872, bapt. 1 Jan 1873 (Baptism, Ballymacelligott & Ballyseedy Parish)

Hurst

William Henry Disney (son):

Residence - Tralee - January 28, 1857

August 19, 1860

December 22, 1861

Bally McElligott Rectory - September 6, 1863

October 6, 1864

October 22, 1871

January 1, 1873

Occupation - Rector of Bally McElligott - January 28, 1857

January 31, 1858

April 22, 1859

December 22, 1861

January 1, 1873

Rector of Ballyseedy - August 19, 1860

Clerk - September 6, 1863

October 22, 1871

Reverend - October 6, 1864

Mary Jane Denny, daughter of Anthony Denny (1st wife) (daughter-in-law):

Residence - Tralee - January 28, 1857

The Rectory, Bally McElligott - September 3, 1864

Occupation - Lady - January 28, 1857

Age at Death - 32 years

Anthony Denny (father):

Signature:

Occupation - Rector of Tralee

Henry Disney (father):

Occupation - Captain of 37th Regiment

Wedding Witnesses:

A. B. Rowan & William Trames

Signatures:

Henry Disney (father):

Residence - No. 3 Whitworth Place - February 1, 1829

April 28, 1831

Occupation - 37th Regiment of Foot - February 1, 1829

Esquire - April 28, 1831

Hurst

- Henry R. E. Disney & Emma P. Disney

  o Kathleen Dora Disney – b. 6 Dec 1886, bapt. 17 Jan 1887 (Baptism, **Irishtown Parish**)

  o Violet Patience Disney – b. 16 Apr 1889, bapt. 19 May 1889 (Baptism, **Irishtown Parish**)

  o Mary Deaney Disney – b. 10 Sep 1890, bapt. 10 Sep 1890 (Baptism, **St. Matthew Parish**)

  o Thomas Brabazon Laurent Disney – b. 26 Jan 1895, bapt. 6 Mar 1895 (Baptism, **St. James Parish**) (Baptism, **St. Matthew Parish**)

Henry R. E. Disney (father):

Residence - Newbridge Avenue - January 17, 1886

20 Claremont Road - May 19, 1889

September 10, 1890

March 6, 1895

Occupation - Esquire - January 17, 1886

May 19, 1889

Solicitor - September 10, 1890

March 6, 1895

- James Disney & Anne Moore – 2 Aug 1818 (Baptism, **St. Mary Parish**)

- James Disney & Martha Disney

  o William Disney – bapt. 13 Aug 1809 (Baptism, **Tullow Parish**)

- John Disney & Mary Disney

  o Henry Disney – bapt. 19 Aug 1814 (Baptism, **St. Mark Parish**)

Disney Surname Ireland: 1600s to 1900s

John Disney (father):

Residence - Moss Street - August 19, 1814

- John Disney & Unknown
  - Elizabeth Disney & Joseph Warren – 20 May 1859 (Marriage, **St. Bride Parish**)

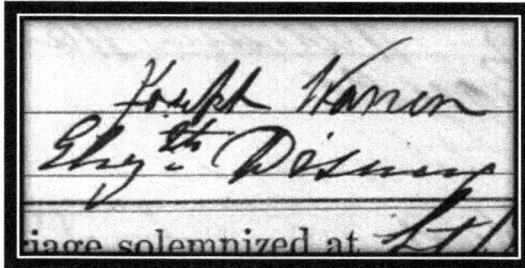

Signatures:

Elizabeth Disney (daughter):

Residence - 28 Bishop Street - May 20, 1859

Joseph Warren, son of William Warren (son-in-law):

Residence - 28 Bishop Street - May 20, 1859

Occupation - Cabinet Maker - May 20, 1859

William Warren (father):

Occupation - Farmer

John Disney (father):

Occupation - Engraver

Hurst

Wedding Witnesses:

Thomas Kenrick & Anne Hall

Signatures:

- Jonathan Disney & Caroline Bren

Signature:

o James Disney & Charlotte Smith – 28 Jan 1875 (Marriage, **St. Peter Parish**)

Signatures:

Disney Surname Ireland: 1600s to 1900s

Signatures (Marriage):

- Florence Elizabeth Disney – b. 19 Dec 1875, bapt. 20 Feb 1876 (Baptism, **St. John Parish**)

- Albert Edward Disney – b. 18 Jun 1878, bapt. 28 Jul 1878 (Baptism, **St. Werburgh Parish**)

- James Lambert Disney – b. 9 Apr 1880, bapt. 16 May 1880 (Baptism, **St. Werburgh Parish**)

James Disney (son):

Residence - 28 Charlemont Street - January 28, 1875

25 Camden Street - February 20, 1876

57 Synge Street - July 28, 1878

May 16, 1880

Occupation - Chandler - January 28, 1875

July 28, 1878

May 16, 1880

Tallow Chandler - February 20, 1876

Charlotte Smith, daughter of Robert Smith (daughter-in-law):

Residence - Chief Secretary's Office, Castle Yard - January 28, 1875

Robert Smith (father):

Occupation - Porter, Chief Secretary Office

Jonathan Disney (father):

Occupation - Chandler

Wedding Witnesses:

Charles G. Smith & Elizabeth Smith

Signatures:

- o   John Disney & Teresa Mary Dunne – 20 Aug 1863 (Marriage, **St. Nicholas Parish** (RC))
    - ▪ Mary Teresa Disney – b. 24 May 1864, bapt. 8 Jun 1864 (Baptism, **St. Nicholas Parish** (RC))

John Disney (son):

Residence - 32 Lower Clanbrassil Street - August 20, 1863

June 8, 1864

Teresa Mary Dunne, daughter of Patrick Dunne & Mary Lynch (daughter-in-law):

Residence - 32 Lower Clanbrassil Street - August 20, 1863

Wedding Witnesses:

John Dunne & Deborah Upton

- o Martha Disney, b. 10 Jul 1840, bapt. 24 Aug 1840 (Baptism, **St. Peter Parish**) & Patrick George

  Dunne – 18 Apr 1870 (Marriage, **St. Peter Parish**)

Signature:

Signatures (Marriage):

Martha Disney (daughter):

Residence - 79 Lower Camden Street - April 18, 1870

Patrick George Dunne, son of Patrick Dunne (son-in-law):

Residence - 69 Lower Camden Street - April 18, 1870

Occupation - Accountant - April 18, 1870

Patrick Dunne (father):

Occupation - Accountant

Jonathan Disney (father):

Occupation - Chandler

Hurst

Wedding Witnesses:

James Disney & Abigail Disney

Signatures:

- o   Caroline Disney, b. 11 Aug 1842, bapt. 25 Aug 1842 (Baptism, **St. Peter Parish**) & Michael Rainsbury Blake – 22 Nov 1864 (Marriage, **St. Peter Parish**)

Signatures:

Caroline Disney (daughter):

Residence - 79 Camden Street - November 22, 1864

Michael Rainsbury Blake, son of Michael Blake (son-in-law):

Residence - Dysart, Castleinch Parish, Co. Kilkenny - November 22, 1864

Occupation - Esquire Secretary to the Earl of Dysart - November 22, 1864

Michael Blake (father):

Occupation - Land Agent

Disney Surname Ireland: 1600s to 1900s

Jonathan Disney (father):

    Residence - Chandler

Wedding Witnesses:

James Disney & Martha Disney

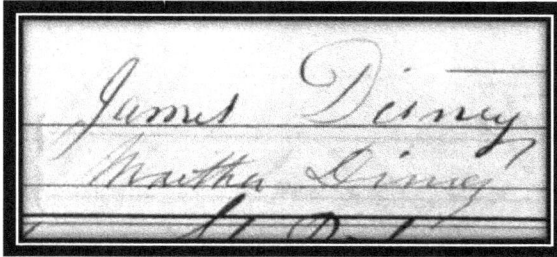

Signatures:

- ○   Samuel Disney – b. 25 Jul 1844, bapt. 11 Aug 1844 (Baptism, **St. Peter Parish**)

- ○   Thomas Rochfort Disney – b. 24 Jan 1846, bapt. 8 Feb 1846 (Baptism, **St. Peter Parish**)

- ○   William Christopher Disney – b. 25 Dec 1847, bapt. 9 Jan 1848 (Baptism, **St. Peter Parish**)

- ○   Abigail Disney, b. 13 Feb 1850, bapt. 3 Mar 1850 (Baptism, **Rathmines Parish**) & John James Regley – 5 Mar 1878 (Marriage, **St. Peter Parish**)

Signature:

Signatures (Marriage):

Abigail Disney (daughter):

    Residence - 18 Charlemont Mall - March 5, 1878

John James Regley, son of John Regley (son-in-law):

    Residence - 23 Emer Street, South Circular Road - March 5, 1878

    Occupation - Commercial Clerk - March 5, 1878

John Regley (father):

    Occupation - Farmer

Jonathan Disney (father):

    Occupation - Chandler

Wedding Witnesses:

Jonathan Disney & Anne Hughes

Signatures:

Disney Surname Ireland: 1600s to 1900s

- Frances Disney – b. 5 Aug 1852, bapt. 1 Sep 1852 (Baptism, **St. George Parish**)

- Charles John Disney – b. 1854, bapt. 1854 (Baptism, **Crumlin Parish**)

Jonathan Disney (father):

Residence - Rathmines - August 24, 1840

Rathmines Avenue - August 25, 1842

August 11, 1844

February 8, 1846

Kimmage Road - January 9, 1848

March 3, 1850

1854

1 North Summer Street - September 1, 1852

Occupation - Chandler - August 25, 1842

August 11, 1844

February 8, 1846

January 9, 1848

March 3, 1850

Tallow Chandler - September 1, 1852

Grocer and Provision Dealer - 1854

Hurst

- Moore Disney & Jane Unknown

  - William Disney – bapt. Jun 1742 (Baptism, **St. Werburgh Parish**)

  - Thomas Disney – bapt. 10 Sep 1743 (Baptism, **St. Werburgh Parish**)

Moore Disney (father):

Residence - Hoey's Court - June 1742

Hoey's Alley - September 10, 1743

- Morris Disney & Esther Disney

  - Robert Disney – b. 19 Jul 1746, bapt. 21 Jul 1746 (Baptism, **St. Mary Parish**)

- Richard Disney & Charlotte Thorpe – 30 Aug 1833 (Marriage, **St. Audoen Parish**) (Marriage, **St. Audoen Parish** (RC))

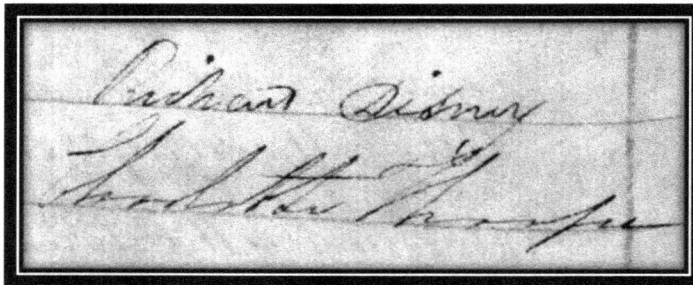

Signatures:

  - Thomas George Disney – b. 21 Jan 1836, bapt. 5 Feb 1836 (Baptism, **Dunleckney Parish**)

  - Richard Disney – b. 23 May 1839, bapt. 8 Feb 1840 (Baptism, **Dunleckney Parish**)

Richard Disney (father):

Residence - Bagenalstown, Co. Carlow - August 30, 1833

Usher's Quay, St. Audoen Parish - August 30, 1833

Bagenalstown - February 8, 1840

Occupation - Shop Keeper - February 8, 1840

Charlotte Thorpe (mother):

Residence - Usher's Quay, St. Audoen Parish - August 30, 1833

Wedding Witnesses:

Thomas Mulhall & Elizabeth Kenna

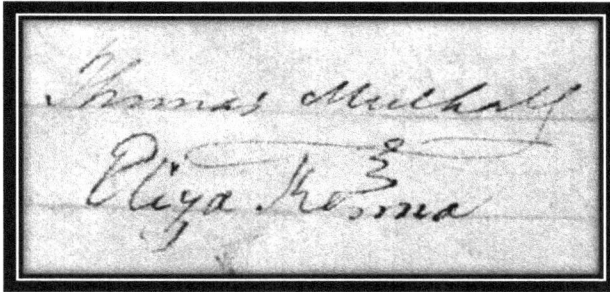

Signatures:

- Robert Disney & Jane Disney

  o Brabazon Disney – b. 7 Sep 1799, bapt. 30 Oct 1799 (Baptism, **Glasnevin Parish**), bur. 28 Mar 1802

    (Burial, **Glasnevin Parish**)

Brabazon Disney (son):

Residence - Glasnevin - before March 28, 1802

  o Harold Disney – b. 30 Oct 1800, bapt. 21 Dec 1800 (Baptism, **Glasnevin Parish**)

  o Lambert Brabazon Disney – b. 6 Sep 1802, bapt. 21 Nov 1802 (Baptism, **Glasnevin Parish**)

  o Jane Disney – b. 23 Oct 1805, bapt. 9 Dec 1805 (Baptism, **Glasnevin Parish**)

  o Robert Disney – b. 25 Jan 1806, bapt. 11 May 1806 (Baptism, **Glasnevin Parish**)

  o Patience Ogle Disney – b. 19 Dec 1806, bapt. 31 Dec 1806 (Baptism, **Glasnevin Parish**)

Hurst

- Robert Disney & Mary Kappell – 2 Feb 1775 (Marriage, **Carlow Parish**)

- Robert Disney & Mary Anne Unknown

  o Louise Disney – b. 15 Jan 1836, bapt. 20 Jan 1836 (Baptism, **St. Peter Parish**) (Baptism, **Clondalkin Parish** (RC))

Robert Disney (father):

Residence - No. 16 Aungier Street - 1836

- Robert Anthony Disney & Caroline Disney

  o Robert Disney – b. 2 Jun 1846, bapt. 2 Jul 1846 (Baptism, **Clontarf Parish**)

  o Caroline Dorothea Disney – b. 20 May 1848, bapt. 21 Jun 1848 (Baptism, **Clontarf Parish**)

  o Catherine Louise Disney – b. 2 Oct 1849, bapt. 26 Oct 1849 (Baptism, **St. Stephen Parish**)

Robert Anthony Disney (father):

Residence - Clontarf - July 2, 1846

June 21, 1848

5 Broughaw Place - October 26, 1849

Occupation - Esquire - July 2, 1846

Solicitor - June 21, 1848

October 26, 1849

- Samuel Disney & Frances Unknown

  o Samuel Disney – bapt. 12 Jul 1812 (Baptism, **St. Mary, Pro Cathedral Parish** (RC))

  o Robert Disney – bapt. 20 Nov 1814 (Baptism, **St. Mary, Pro Cathedral Parish** (RC))

  o Frances Disney – bapt. 20 Apr 1818 (Baptism, **St. Mary, Pro Cathedral Parish** (RC))

- o Teresa Disney – bapt. 18 Oct 1819 (Baptism, **St. Mary, Pro Cathedral Parish (RC)**)

Samuel Disney (father):

Residence - North Strand - April 20, 1818

October 18, 1819

- Samuel Disney & Mary Disney
  - o Francis Disney – bapt. 19 Apr 1780 (Baptism, **St. Mark Parish**)

Samuel Disney (father):

Residence - George's Street - April 19, 1780

- Samuel Disney & Sarah Disney
  - o Samuel Disney – bapt. 18 Dec 1782 (Baptism, **St. Mark Parish**)

Samuel Disney (father):

Residence - Hawks Street - December 18, 1782

- Samuel Disney & Sarah Magee – 14 Nov 1777 (Marriage, **St. Bride Parish**)

Samuel Disney (husband):

Occupation - Gentleman - November 14, 1777

Sarah Magee (wife):

Occupation - Spinster - November 14, 1777

- Theobald Disney & Catherine Travers – 6 Mar 1761 (Marriage, **St. Mark Parish**)
- Thomas Disney & Anne Shea – 17 Nov 1808 (Marriage, **St. Mary Parish**)

Hurst

- Thomas Disney & Anne Elizabeth Disney

  - William John Disney – b. 29 Feb 1796, bapt. 29 Feb 1796 (Baptism, **Glasnevin Parish**)

  - Lambert Disney – b. 26 Jul 1808, bapt. 28 Aug 1808 (Baptism, **Glasnevin Parish**)

- Thomas Disney & Catherine Fox – 1846 (Marriage, **Rathmines Parish (RC)**)

  - George Disney – bapt. 9 Jun 1850 (Baptism, **Rathmines Parish (RC)**)

Wedding Witnesses:

Thomas Farren & Margaret Moran

- Thomas Disney & Catherine Unknown

  - Lawrence Disney & Jane Johnson – 18 Apr 1869 (Marriage, **St. Andrew Parish (RC)**)

Lawrence Disney (son):

Residence - Ring's End - April 18, 1869

Jane Johnson, daughter of Augustine Johnson & Catherine Unknown (daughter-in-law):

Residence - 11 Merrion Row - April 18, 1869

Wedding Witnesses:

Michael Disney & Mary Fox

- Thomas Disney & Elizabeth Disney

  - Frances Anne Disney – b. 8 Oct 1826, bapt. 29 Oct 1826 (Baptism, **Tullow Parish**)

  - James Disney – b. 13 Oct 1827, bapt. 11 Nov 1827 (Baptism, **Tullow Parish**)

- Thomas Disney & Elizabeth Taylor – 8 Oct 1728 (Baptism, **St. Luke Parish**)

Disney Surname Ireland: 1600s to 1900s

Thomas Disney (husband):

Residence - St. Bride Parish - October 8, 1728

Elizabeth Taylor (wife):

Residence - St. Luke Parish - October 8, 1728

- Thomas Disney & Frances Ashe – 7 Jan 1831 (Marriage, **St. Audoen Parish**)

Signatures:

Thomas Disney (husband):

Residence - Kill, Co. Carlow - January 7, 1831

Usher's Quay, St. Audoen Parish - January 7, 1831

Frances Thorpe (wife):

Residence - Usher's Quay, St. Audoen Parish - January 7, 1831

Occupation - Spinster - January 7, 1831

Wedding Witnesses:

George Ashe & Benjamin Dill

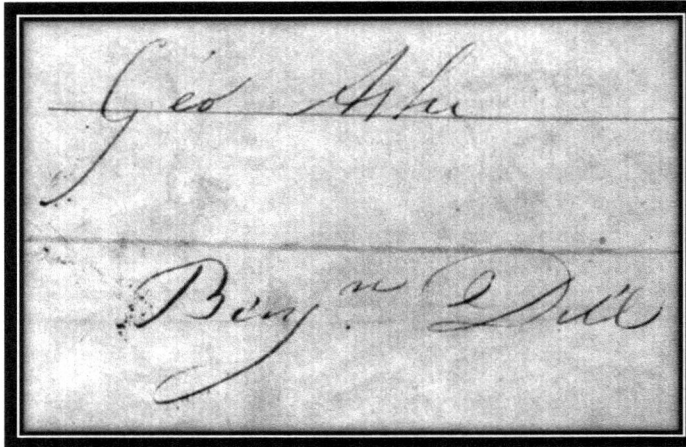

Signatures:

- Thomas Disney & Margaret Disney

  - George Disney – bapt. 30 Jan 1692 (Baptism, **St. Michan Parish**)

Thomas Disney (father):

Occupation - Saddler - January 30, 1692

- Thomas Disney & Martha Wilkinson – 4 Jun 1774 (Marriage, **St. Andrew Parish**)

- Thomas Disney & Mary Unknown

  - Robert Disney – bapt. 10 Mar 1669 (Baptism, **St. Peter Parish**)

  - Thomas Disney – bapt. 31 May 1674 (Baptism, **St. Peter Parish**)

- Unknown Disney & Unknown

  - Anne Disney – b. 9 Oct 1841, bur. 12 Oct 1841 (Burial, **St. Mark Parish**)

Disney Surname Ireland: 1600s to 1900s

Anne Disney (daughter):

Residence - Gardner Street - before October 12, 1841

Age at Death - 3 days

- o   Jane Disney – b. 9 Oct 1841, bur. 12 Oct 1841 (Burial, **St. Mark Parish**)

Jane Disney (daughter):

Residence - Gardner Street - before October 12, 1841

Age at Death - 3 days

- Unknown Disney & Unknown
  - o   Charles Disney

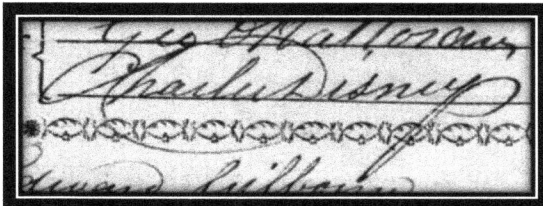

Signature:

- Unknown Disney & Unknown
  - o   Eli E. Disney

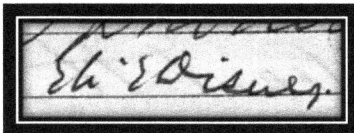

Signature:

- Unknown Disney & Unknown

  o Ellen G. Disney

Signature:

- Unknown Disney & Unknown

  o Francis Disney

Signature:

- Unknown Disney & Unknown

  o Francis Disney

Signature:

- Unknown Disney & Unknown

  o James Disney

Signature:

- Unknown Disney & Unknown

  o James Wemys Arthur Disney

Signatures:

- Unknown Disney & Unknown

  o Julie Disney

Signature:

- Unknown Disney & Unknown

  o Unknown Disney & Anne Unknown (1st Marriage)

  o Anne Unknown Disney (2nd Marriage) & John Warren – 31 Jul 1824 (Marriage, **St. Mary Parish**)

Anne Unknown Disney (wife):

Residence - St. Mary Parish - July 31, 1824

Relationship Status at Marriage - widow

John Warren (husband):

Residence - Tullow, Co. Carlow - July 31, 1824

Wedding Witnesses:

James Moore, George Warren, & Robert Stephens

- Unknown Disney & Unknown

  o Unknown Disney & Sarah Unknown (1st Marriage)

  o Sarah Unknown Disney (2nd Marriage) & Richard Pickhaver – 3 Nov 1793 (Marriage, **St. Bride Parish**)

Disney Surname Ireland: 1600s to 1900s

Sarah Unknown Disney (wife):

    Relationship Status at Marriage - widow

- William Disney & Anne Oliver – 29 Feb 1804 (Marriage, **St. Peter Parish**)

- William Disney & Jane Roe

  o William Disney – b. 6 Nov 1825, bapt. 6 Nov 1825 (Baptism, **Kilcolman Parish**)

William Disney (father):

    Residence - Miltown - November 6, 1825

    Occupation - Reverend Officer - November 6, 1825

- William Disney & Unknown

  o Ellen Disney, b. 1825 & Michael Mansfield, b. 1824 – 6 Jul 1847 (Marriage, **Carlow Parish**)

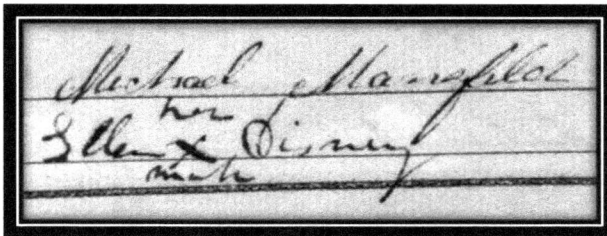

Signatures:

Ellen Disney (daughter):

    Residence - Carlow - July 6, 1847

    Occupation - House Keeper - July 6, 1847

    Age at Marriage - 22 years

Hurst

Michael Mansfield, son of Michael Mansfield (son-in-law):

Residence - Carlow - July 6, 1847

Occupation - Miller - July 6, 1847

Age at Marriage - 23 years

Michael Mansfield (father):

Occupation - Taylor

William Disney (father):

Occupation - Pensioner

Wedding Witnesses:

William Disney & Richard Carraher

Signatures:

- William Disney & Unknown
  - Elizabeth Jane Disney & John Higginbotham – 28 Dec 1892 (Marriage, **St. Michan Parish**)

Signatures:

Disney Surname Ireland: 1600s to 1900s

Elizabeth Jane Disney (daughter):

Residence - Inns Quay, Dublin - December 28, 1892

John Higginbotham, son of James Higginbotham (son-in-law):

Residence - Athenry - December 28, 1892

Occupation - Telegraphist - December 28, 1892

James Higginbotham (father):

Occupation - Saddler

William Disney (father):

Occupation - General Manager Solicitor Buildings

Wedding Witnesses:

W. R. Higginbotham & Charlotte Kathleen Disney

Signatures:

- Charlotte Kathleen Disney & Charles Henry Farmer – 1 Aug 1894 (Marriage, **St. Werburgh Parish**)

Signature:

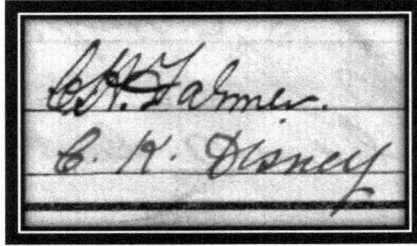

Signatures (Marriage):

Charlotte Kathleen Disney (daughter):

    Residence - Four Courts - August 1, 1894

Charles Henry Farmer, son of William Farmer (son-in-law):

    Residence - Wellington Quay - August 1, 1894

    Occupation - Dentist - August 1, 1894

William Farmer (father):

    Occupation - Clerk

William Disney (father):

    Occupation - General Manager Solicitor's Buildings

Wedding Witnesses:

William Farmer & S. J. Farmer

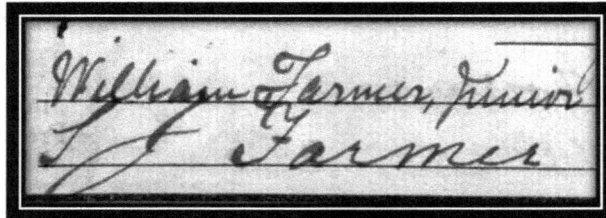

Signatures:

o John George Disney & Elizabeth Sarah Clark Atkinson – 24 Jan 1899 (Marriage, **St. Werburgh Parish**)

Signatures:

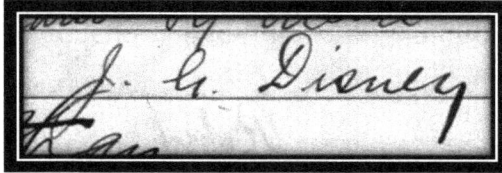

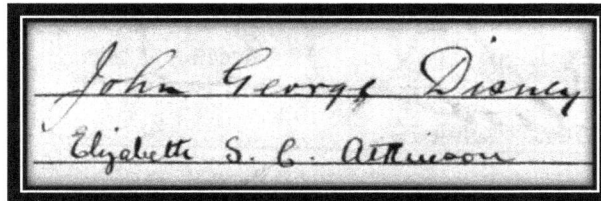

Signatures (Marriage):

John George Disney (son):

Residence - Portlaw - January 24, 1899

Occupation - Clerk in Holy Orders, M. A. - January 24, 1899

Elizabeth Sarah Clark Atkinson, daughter of Samuel Atkinson (daughter-in-law):

Residence - Sloan's Hotel, Dublin - January 24, 1899

Samuel Atkinson (father):

Occupation - Clerk in Holy Orders

William Disney (father):

Occupation - General Manager Incorporated Law Society Ireland

Wedding Witnesses:

Herbert M. C. Hughes & Jane L. Atkinson

Signatures:

- William Doherty Disney & Anne Doherty Disney
    - William Doherty Disney – b. 26 Jan 1879, bapt. 13 Mar 1879 (Baptism, **St. Peter Parish**)

William Doherty Disney (father):

Residence - 11 Synge Place - March 13, 1879

Occupation - Sailor - March 13, 1879

Individual Baptisms/Births

- Abigail Disney – bapt. 27 Sep 1821 (Baptism, **Tullow Parish**)

- Henry Disney – bapt. Apr 1824 (Baptism, **St. Mark Parish**)

Henry Disney (child):

   Residence - Westland Row - April 1824

- James Disney – bapt. Apr 1824 (Baptism, **St. Mark Parish**)

James Disney (child):

   Residence - Westland Row - April 1824

- John Disney – bapt. 27 Sep 1821 (Baptism, **Tullow Parish**)

- Richard Disney – bapt. 30 May 1856 (Baptism, **St. Mary, Pro Cathedral Parish** (RC))

Richard Disney (child):

   Residence - 28 Lower Mecklenburgh - May 30, 1856

   Age at Baptism - adult

Individual Burials

- Abigail Disney – b. 1776, bur. 3 Jul 1842 (Burial, **St. Matthew Parish**)

Abigail Disney (deceased):

  Residence - Irishtown - before July 3, 1842

  Age at Death - 66 years

- Alice Disney – bur. 10 Apr 1790 (Burial, **St. Peter Parish**)

Alice Disney (deceased):

  Residence - Phibsborough - before April 10, 1790

  Place of Burial - St. Kevin's Cemetery

- Anne Disney – bur. 18 Jan 1751 (Burial, **St. Mark Parish**)

- Brabazon Disney – bur. 3 Nov 1780 (Burial, **St. Paul Parish**)

- Brabazon Disney – b. 1801, bur. 28 Mar 1853 (Burial, **St. Paul Parish**)

Brabazon Disney (deceased):

  Age at Death - 52 years

- Caroline Disney – b. 1810, bur. 18 Jun 1839 (Burial, **St. Mark Parish**)

Caroline Disney (deceased):

  Residence - Sea Point - before June 18, 1839

  Age at Death - 29 years

Disney Surname Ireland: 1600s to 1900s

- Caroline Disney – b. 1811, bur. 17 Feb 1855 (Burial, **St. Mark Parish**)

Caroline Disney (deceased):

  Residence - Seafield Terrace, Donnybrook - before February 17, 1855

  Age at Death - 44 years

- Catherine Disney – b. 1804, bur. 17 Dec 1864 (Burial, **St. Paul Parish**)

Catherine Disney (deceased):

  Residence - Glenarm, Co., Antrim - before December 17, 1864

  Age at Death - 60 years

- Edward George Disney – b. 1812, bur. 18 Jan 1854 (Burial, **St. Mark Parish**)

Edward George Disney (deceased):

  Residence - 75 Aungier Street - before January 18, 1854

  Age at Death - 42 years

- Elizabeth Disney – bur. 18 Jan 1697 (Burial, **St. Michan Parish**)
- Elizabeth Disney – bur. 14 Feb 1799 (Burial, **St. Peter Parish**)

Elizabeth Disney (deceased):

  Residence - Northumberland Street - before February 14, 1799

Hurst

- Frances Disney – b. 1839, bur. 26 Feb 1862 (Burial, **St. Mark Parish**)

Frances Disney (deceased):

    Residence - 28 Leinster Square, Rathmines - before February 26, 1862

    Age at Death - 23 years

- Frances Disney – b. 1795, bur. 6 Nov 1877 (Burial, **St. Paul Parish**)

Frances Disney (deceased):

    Residence - Glenarm, Co. Antrim - before November 6, 1877

    Age at Death - 82 years

- Jane Disney – bur. 28 Mar 1768 (Burial, **St. Paul Parish**)

Jane Disney (deceased):

    Residence - Queen Street - before March 28, 1768

- John Disney – bur. 30 Nov 1807 (Burial, **Irishtown Parish**)

John Disney (deceased):

    Residence - Ring's End - before November 30, 1807

    Occupation - Revenue Officer - before November 30, 1807

- John Disney – b. 1796, bur. 11 Apr 1836 (Burial, **St. Peter Parish**)

John Disney (deceased):

    Residence - Aungier Street - before April 11, 1836

    Age at Death - 40 years

Disney Surname Ireland: 1600s to 1900s

- Jon Disney – bur. 6 Mar 1702 (Burial, **St. Nicholas Without Parish**)

Jon Disney (deceased):

    Residence - Francis Street - before March 6, 1702

- Mary Disney – b. 1767, bur. 14 Feb 1839 (Burial, **Dunleckney Parish**)

Mary Disney (deceased):

    Residence - Carlow - before February 14, 1839

- Mary Anne Disney – b. 1815, bur. 25 Apr 1836 (Burial, **St. Peter Parish**)

Mary Anne Disney (deceased):

    Residence - Aungier Street - before April 25, 1836

    Age at Death - 21 years

- Patience Disney – bur. 20 May 1770 (Burial, **St. Paul Parish**)

Patience Disney (deceased):

    Residence - Queen Street - before May 20, 1770

- Patience Disney – bur. 30 Aug 1807 (Burial, **St. Peter Parish**)

Patience Disney (deceased):

    Residence - Holles Street - before August 30, 1807

- Richard Disney – bur. 19 Jan 1773 (Burial, **St. Paul Parish**)

Richard Disney (deceased):

    Residence - Green Street - before January 19, 1773

Hurst

- Theobald Disney – bur. 29 Apr 1774 (Burial, **St. Paul Parish**)

- Theobald Disney – bur. 3 Mar 1785 (Burial, **St. Paul Parish**)

Theobald Disney (deceased):

  Occupation - Reverend - before March 3, 1785

- Unknown Disney – bur. 13 Dec 1700 (Burial, **St. Peter Parish**)

Unknown Disney (deceased):

  Residence - Avery Water - before December 13, 1700

- Unknown Disney – bur. 27 Jan 1790 (Burial, **St. Peter Parish**)

Unknown Disney (deceased):

  Residence - Hume Street - before January 27, 1790

  Place of Burial - St. Peter's Cemetery

- Unknown Disney – bur. 12 Nov 1797 (Burial, **St. Peter Parish**)

Unknown Disney (deceased):

  Residence - Abbey Street – before November 12, 1797

- Unknown Disney – bur. 1 Jan 1807 (Burial, **Glasnevin Parish**)

Unknown Disney (deceased):

  Remarks about Burial - church register entry lists individual as Master Disney.

- Unknown Disney (Mrs.) – bur. 6 Dec 1759 (Burial, **St. Mary Parish**)

Disney Surname Ireland: 1600s to 1900s

Individual Marriages

- Abigail Disney & Anthony Rainsford – 1 Nov 1825 (Marriage, **Tullow Parish**)

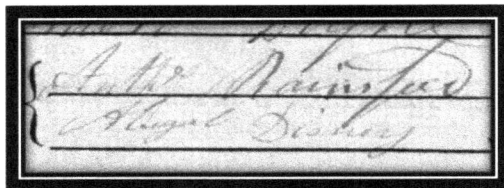

Signatures:

Abigail Disney (wife):

Residence - Tullow - November 1, 1825

Anthony Rainsford (husband):

Residence - St. Anne Parish, Co. Dublin - November 1, 1825

Wedding Witnesses:

Thomas Disney & Abigail Rainsford

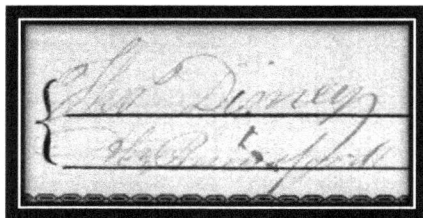

Signatures:

- Anne Disney & Henry Grove – 24 Apr 1822 (Marriage, **St. Peter Parish**)

Anne Disney (wife):

Residence - St. Peter Parish - April 24, 1822

Disney Surname Ireland: 1600s to 1900s

Henry Grove (husband):

   Residence - St. Peter Parish - April 24, 1822

   Occupation - Lieutenant Colonel - April 24, 1822

Wedding Witnesses:

J. J. Fraser & Robert Ashcroft

- Anne Disney & John Purcell – 9 Feb 1849 (Marriage, **St. Catherine Parish** (RC))

Wedding Witnesses:

Elizabeth Murphy & Ambrose C. Doyle

- Anne Disney & Loghlan Nowlan – 1 Jan 1828 (Marriage, **St. Mary, Pro Cathedral Parish** (RC))

Wedding Witnesses:

Sarah Magrath & Margaret Murtagh

- Anne Jeanne Disney & Richard Gore Daly
  - Anne Jeanne Daly – bapt. 11 Oct 1862 (Baptism, **St. Mary, Pro Cathedral Parish** (RC))
  - Richard Daly – bapt. 5 Jan 1863 (Baptism, **St. Mary, Pro Cathedral Parish** (RC))

Richard Gore Daly (father):

   Residence - 70 Talbot Street - October 11, 1862

       55 Marlboro Street - January 5, 1863

- Catherine Disney & William Barker – 5 May 1825 (Marriage, **St. Mark Parish**)

Signatures:

Catherine Disney (wife):

   Residence - St. Mark Parish - May 5, 1825

William Barker (husband):

   Residence - St. George Parish - May 5, 1825

Wedding Witnesses:

Thomas Disney & James Barlow

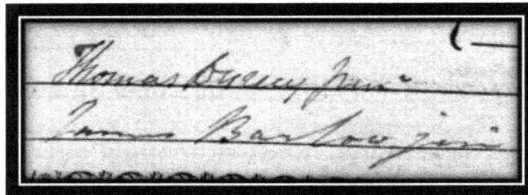

Signatures:

- Charlotte Disney & John Leland MacQuay – 14 Jan 1794 (Marriage, **St. Anne Parish**)
- Eleanor Anne Disney & George Mahood – 18 Aug 1843 (Marriage, **St. Audoen Parish**)

Disney Surname Ireland: 1600s to 1900s

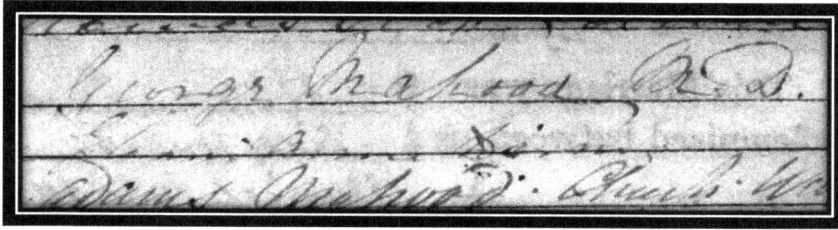

Signatures:

Eleanor Anne Disney (wife):

Residence - South Frederick Street, St. Anne Parish, Dublin - August 18, 1843

George Mahood (husband):

Residence - Upper Bridge Street, St. Audoen Parish - August 1843

Coote Hill, Co. Cavan - August 18, 1843

Occupation - Medical Doctor - August 18, 1843

Wedding Witnesses:

Adams Mahood & Allan Edward Mahood

Signatures:

- Eleanor M. Disney & David Paley

  o Sarah G. Paley – b. 15 Nov 1870, bapt. 24 Nov 1870 (Baptism, **Rathmines Parish** (RC))

  o Christine M. Paley – b. 19 Dec 1871, bapt. 23 Dec 1871 (Baptism, **Rathmines Parish** (RC))

  o David Paley – b. 21 Apr 1873, bapt. 28 Apr 1873 (Baptism, **Rathmines Parish** (RC))

  o Mary J. J. Paley – b. 2 May 1874, bapt. 9 May 1874 (Baptism, **Rathmines Parish** (RC))

Hurst

David Paley (father):

Residence - Adelaide Road - November 24, 1870

April 28, 1873

May 9, 1874

December 23, 1871

- Elizabeth Disney & John Carden – 17 Apr 1765 (Marriage, **St. Bride Parish**)

Elizabeth Disney (wife):

Occupation - Spinster - April 17, 1765

John Carden (husband):

Occupation - Esquire - April 17, 1765

- Ellen Disney & Thomas Whiting
  - Anne Mary Whiting – bapt. 20 Sep 1833 (Baptism, **Skibbereen (Creagh & Sullon) Parish** (RC))
  - William Whiting – bapt. 10 Mar 1846 (Baptism, **Skibbereen (Creagh & Sullon) Parish** (RC))
  - Margaret Whiting – bapt. 26 Sep 1852 (Baptism, **Skibbereen (Creagh & Sullon) Parish** (RC))
  - Jane Whiting – bapt. 13 Oct 1855 (Baptism, **Skibbereen (Creagh & Sullon) Parish** (RC))

Thomas Whiting (father):

Residence - Carrigfadda - September 26, 1852

October 13, 1855

Disney Surname Ireland: 1600s to 1900s

- Jane Disney & Charles Cambie – 15 Jun 1827 (Marriage, **St. Peter Parish**)

Jane Disney (wife):

    Residence - Harcourt Street - June 15, 1827

    Occupation - Spinster - June 15, 1827

Charles Cambie (husband):

    Residence - Brookfield, Kilbarron Parish, Co. Tipperary - June 15, 1827

    Occupation - Esquire - June 15, 1827

Wedding Witnesses:

Alexander Disney & Benjamin Towers

- Jane Disney & John Barlow – 19 Oct 1813 (Marriage, **Clontarf Parish**)

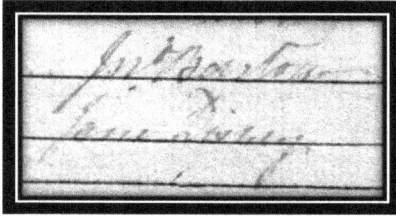

Signatures:

Jane Disney (wife):

    Residence - Clontarf - October 19, 1813

John Barlow (husband):

    Residence - Clontarf - October 19, 1813

Hurst

Wedding Witnesses:

Jane Mansfield, Robert Disney, & Alice Mary Madden

Signatures:

- Louise Disney & Gelverton O'Keefe – 6 Apr 1832 (Marriage, **St. Peter Parish**)

Louise Disney (wife):

Residence - Harcourt Street - April 6, 1832

Occupation - Spinster - April 6, 1832

Gelverton O'Keefe (husband):

Residence - Diswellstown, Castleknock - April 6, 1832

Wedding Witnesses:

Thomas Bakley & John O'Conner

- Mary Disney & John Tomson – 15 Apr 1658 (Marriage, **St. Michael Parish**)
- Mary Ellen Disney & Andrew Reid – 23 Apr 1827 (Marriage, **St. George Parish**)

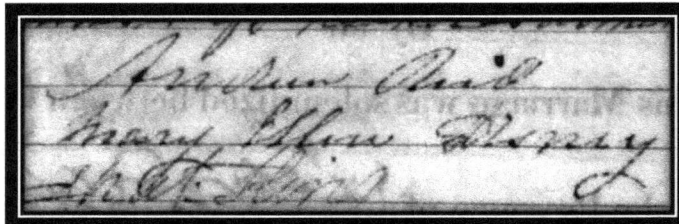

Signatures:

Disney Surname Ireland: 1600s to 1900s

Mary Ellen Disney (wife):

    Residence - St. George Parish - April 23, 1827

Andrew Reid (husband):

    Residence - St. Thomas Parish - April 23, 1827

Wedding Witnesses:

W. Prosser, Charles King, W. Disney, & William Powell

Signatures:

- Sarah Disney & Peter Batchier – 12 Aug 1801 (Marriage, **St. Andrew Parish (RC)**)

Wedding Witnesses:

John Disney & Thomas Morris

- Sophie Disney & Lawrence Dunne – 15 Feb 1825 (Marriage, **St. Peter Parish**)

Sophia Disney (wife):

    Residence - St. Peter Parish - February 15, 1825

Lawrence Dunne (husband):

    Residence - Breefield, Ballycara - February 15, 1825

Wedding Witnesses:

William Disney & John Dunne

Name Variations

Includes Latin and Abbreviated forms of names found in the original documents.

Abigail = Abigale, Abigall

Anne = Ann, Anna, Annae

Bartholomew = Barth, Bartholmeus, Bartholomeo

Bridget = Birgis, Brigid, Brigida, Bridgit

Catherine = Catharine, Catharina, Catharinae, Catherina, Cath, Catha, Cathae, Cathe, Cathn, Kate

Charles = Carolus, Charls, Chas

Christopher = Christoph

Daniel = Danielem, Danielis

Edmund = Edmond

Edward = Ed, Edwd

Eleanor = Eleo, Eleonora, Elinor, Ellenor

Elizabeth = Betty, Elisa, Elisabeth, Eliz, Eliza, Elizab, Elizh, Elizth

Ellen = Elena, Ellena

Emily = Emilia

Esther = Essie, Ester

Francis = Fransicum

George = Geo, Georg, Georgius

Grace = Gratiae

Gulielmo = Guil, Guillelmi, Gulielmum, Guillelmus, Gulmi

Helen = Helena

Disney Surname Ireland: 1600s to 1900s

Honor = Hanora, Honora

James = Jacobi, Jacobus, Jas

Jane = Joanna

Jeanne = Jeannae, Joannae

Joan = Johanna, Joney

John = Jno, Joannem, Joannes, Johannis

Joseph = Jos

Juliana = Julian

Leticia = Letitia, Lettice, Letticia

Lewis = Louis

Luke = Lucas

Margaret = Margarita, Margaritae, Margeret, Marget, Margt

Martha = Marthae

Mary = Maria, My

Mary Anne = Marianna, Marianne, Maryanne

Michael = Michaelis, Michl

Patrick = Pat, Patt, Patk, Patricii, Patricius

Peter = Petri

Richard = Ricardi, Ricardus, Rich, Richd

Robert = Roberti

Rose = Rosa, Rosae

Thomas = Thom, Thomae, Thoms, Thos, Ths

Timothy = Timotheus, Timy

William = Wil, Will, Willm, Wm

Notes

Notes

Notes

Notes

Notes

Notes

Index

Disney Surname Ireland: 1600s to 1900s

Hurst

Disney Surname Ireland: 1600s to 1900s

About The Author

Donovan Hurst graduated from San Diego State University with a Bachelor of Arts in the major field of studies of History and a minor in the field of studies of Anthropology. He is a current member of The General Society of Mayflower Descendants and has been conducting genealogical research for over 10 years tracing back his ancestors to their ancestral homelands in Denmark, England, France, Germany, Ireland, Norway, and Scotland.

www.ingramcontent.com/pod-product-compliance
Lightning Source LLC
Chambersburg PA
CBHW081200270326

41930CB00014B/3227